AF480038

AN AMERICAN TRAGEDY

Hello, I am Lan Main. An American Tragedy takes you on a journey of joy, heartache, confusion, murder, and death. The book itself was written in a few months, but it contains work that spreads out from multiple years. Some poems featured were written as young as I was 13. The motive of the book is sewed together in a flow-like state of expression. While this is my work, it was barely "hard" work and these poems were written at first without any intention of publication. Many of the words in this book were just late night ideas that made it hard to sleep, things that haunt me. What you read is my sight, my feelings, my figures, seen injustices, stitched together philosophies, and world views. I'd like to consider myself positive, but I cannot deny most of…if not all of these poems contain sadness and melancholy. Most of it is from personal experience, but mixed in it all are stories of the past and now that aren't mine, yet bother me no less. In order to truly appreciate the wonder of life you must soak in and filter disgusting deprived corners of humanity in order to cleanse them with your sponge heart. What is untalked of, continues. Remember, it is a slippery privilege to even talk of such things. This book of poetry is to honor love, and honor the dead. I hope it touches your soul and reminds you to live a life to respect and help others.

Before The States

Let me set this straight
do not hate everything about the states.
Yet everyone makes mistakes
History is not made by saints
Privileged to not make this with paints
Yet what is this gift from?
Has the worst even come?
The first hailing from land bridge
Clovis from now Alaska
Not at disadvantage
Will be taken advantaged
Notice the natured land so full
Tall trees and creatures now extinct
Will it be gone with a blink?
North to South never ending mystery
So many habitats and lost history
Imagine the scents from the plants
Animals not calling out in distress
Green on brown on blue sky
Desert a warm toasted fry
The moist dirt so fertile
Flowers so horny
pines tall with authority
Cliffs royal marble
Bare feet feeling
Feeling naked yet safe
Feeling earth's motherly embrace
Aware of the cell you once were
Aware of the space dust inside
Reside with babyish innocence
With the chill grass…
Drip. Drip.
Did you just step on glass…?

Big tech trying to get out of the universe
Ticking timer around us
And I like the constructedness
I'm usually feeling useless
But today I'm going to watch the sun
Never lasts forever, I know far too well
Standing in a empty space
The picture im holding can last forever
My soul was made to be battered by you
Queue the idealistic victory
Never ending in tragedy
Pushing towards a better world
No amount of makeup faces can replace
The rocky face
I think i'm going to keep your space
Nice and tidy for return
Take me where there are people
And hysterical laughter booming
Though after, sit and reflect it wasn't with you
Today i'm going to watch the sun
Let it consume me
Dangerous warmth
Everyone is holding hands today
Or let the sun go away
But everything will be so cold
We'd have to abandon our home
And my soul was made to be battered by you
Ticking timer
I can make it last forever

You opened your blue eyes I was quite surprised
Eyes like a pool I'd like to dive into
Your diamond eyes shine like the most delicious drink
Or the deepest natural water spring
I was blind to them before
But I won't be anymore
Did you know the eyes are the portal to the soul?
I'll swim into them so I can meet your mind
It hurts not being closer
It hurts worser
But I can picture your blue eyes letting me in
So I can understand
Be close love
You are a heartthrob dove
Putting me on a kabob
I know you don't got no time for a man
I'll prove to you I can
Your looking so good
The girl I dreamed of since boyhood
I can't be no shag
No ragtag, I gotta keep it cool
Not drool like the other guys
Can't you see it in my eyes?

I am immeasurably troubled
I cannot describe their soul I adore
They are a cushioned brown filter
My pink sketched rose
They are a strawberry shortcake
My old painting of urban France
They are the smell of children books
My Victorian advert queen
They are a old love song dance
My gentle heartache melody
They are a green vine on red bricks
My foggy city yellow morning glow
They are coffee and jazz
My banana bread and tea smell
They are a field of sunflowers
My lady bug
They are red lipstick stains
My cherry burgundy jewel
They are a box of old vinyl
My hippie glass shine
They are slow as passionate soul sound
My piano fem class
They are everything resplendent
I took a picture
Thought they'd be the best model
I came up with a character
It was based off them
I wrote a song
It was their life
I drew a face

It looked just like them
I am immeasurably troubled
I cannot describe how
Their skin sits upon muscle making their distinguished gaze
Something that shall never be made again
This is my foolish and wild
Confession of flowered manic love
That I believe to only feel
Radiating with a glow
That would recognize them
In a completely different body
I am immeasurably troubled
I cannot describe their soul I adore

You wouldn't believe the deprivation I've seen
Too much blood on the tv screen
Troubled man I knew
His sister stabbed her own
Snuffed the infant
Postpartum-psychosis
How are you supposed to explain this?
The animalistic whines of terror
I dreamed in a space of pure sorrow
Truth is stranger than fiction
My modor swore she met her in jail
But I know it was some tale
For a year after she was hung in a prison cell
 How are you supposed to explain this
To an eight year old?
Someone meant to protect
Almost kills you then hangs
The mind numbing ghoulish horror
Emotions of morbidity, too much carnage
I cried when I heard
They found a child nude in the forest
Cuts in her cake flesh, dirt in her cuts
Grown beast violated her
I was lit on fire to avenge an angel
Raw emotion to kill a sicko
Walking to school she sees future
He watched from the window
The open grave of a body you loved
The skin so cold you held on Christmas fires…
Just layers of makeup mannequin
open wounds entered by a grotesque member
The wailing screams of a mother, "My Daughter!"
When will hell be too full?

Practice forgiveness they say, I like the thought of a saint
How many lives will the sickos keep on living
How did a baby born so sweet?
Become a mind so diseased?
What were they taught to believe?
You wouldn't believe the deprivation I've heard!

You sat there
Around his neck, to peck his cheek
And you wanted life so sweet
Floating in the shallow water
In a concrete basement
Her white dressed covered in blood
She never deserved that payment
Her pale face so content
Some forgotten rusty wall
Touching dirt and dead grass
In infant snowless winter days
My tears drop onto her sunken bags
It now looks she is crying
I hold the bean bag body carefully
And I sob more
A primal sob from deep within
Chains rattling with a echo
We sit in the shallow basement water
What was the last thing you felt?
I'll try to remind you of warmth
Squeezing you with all my force
Yet she is at peace
Simply went to sleep
Like a cozy chinese street bar
Seasonal noodles and buzzing led lights
Rosy around flavorful busy sounds
I dont have the heart to bury your sweet face

Origami Factory

He was a curious child Staring at the origami arrangement
His eyes intent on patterns
The perfection like the factory in the distance
Expansion so fast
Paint, pen, dance, sound
All from a flat screen
So convenient
It's all inbound
No need to run around
Living in the future
High tech so super
It's all going to rupture
Like 50 years ago
Like 100 years ago
Like 150 years ago
Like 1,500 years ago
A million years ago
Flesh on meal, no need to be gentle
No need to settle
It's all at your fingertip
Everyone is a god
Immerse into a witch craft world
Robots on a flagship
Occurrences of atmosphere so odd
This is the real world
Fantasy is reality
Engineers are a genie
I'm born into the new world
It's all something to behold
Witnessing the end of a grounded mold

Don't listen
From one you wouldn't take advice
Those who waste their life
They don't know how to cry
So they scream inside
People like you
Speak so low of those who do
Don't get hurt from words
It's just their screaming leaking
Only focus on one trait of you
They don't know, they play victim
They are uncomfortable for your existence
Due to low IQ
We speak so low of those who do
Brandon says he will, "never accept no gay grandson"
Dinah says wear a longer skirt, "I can see your vagina"
Rebecca just popped opioids so she can feel mega
Jack his entire life will never leave his shack
Tell me why these people make you upset

Woke up this morning and my neck hurt
Been making playing around with rope
Made myself choke, Yeah I want to croak
The wilting flowers in my eyes
The static flow in my heart
I made myself a death rope
And it felt so good to choke
Something dark is in my heart
Hearing the sirens
And the baby screams
The people surround and say what happened to it
Pulsed awake with a shock
It's the cries of the damned
All the children slammed
All the cooked
All the fucking crooks
The cycle of working
When I want to be creating
Should of been a doctor
Actually save the world
The rope made me feel safe
Like your beautiful face
Away from the horrors of the human race
As it shines in purple light a party she laughs
I like the way she smiles and shakes her hair
But she dares with some man that has loser hair
I dont need drugs, affection, or false hope
All I need is a rope

Red Dot

I see her travel from the red dot
Asks for a lost card, have I found it?
In a hard purple bag was all she had
I know she didn't lose no credit
And she looked at me so lost
So long she'd been forgot
Walked away again
I see her walk back from the red dot
She sits and begins conversation
With no one there
Customers said it was all crazy talk
All within the mind a creation
I offer to buy her a meal
And she looked at me so lost
So long she'd been forgot
She said no and walked away again
I check the sanitation box
Found syringes
So that is why she is so thin
As she goes again to the red dot
Don't give in
Found frozen in a body bag
Just another old hag
Lost her head
Found dead

Meaningless Genius

You related to every word said
Because not everyone is brain dead
What the tops say isn't meaningless
But it's far from genius
It's all been done before
To settle the score
Mediocrity sustained
To be entertained
Not for your gain
It's all modern aged
The gain you achieve
But still grieve
A few seconds on the screen
So re-printable
We don't need another one making girls scream
 We don't need another failed criminal
Or another that sings about fleshy kinks so liminal
Be yourself yet we are all akin
Same under the skin
When people give you no respect
Be intelligent, because when you are ignorant
You get treated that way
And when you are bashed and judged got nothing to say
Leading to another numerous grudge
Because the tops are only just "that"
Till another copies and acts like a brat

Killed your potential
Made your opportunities confidential
A cog in a factory
Yet still a worker so thirsty
Blue or Red set a divide
They got you tied to decide
Socialists can only be so left
Damned get food, still be theft
It is a working engine
On blood fuel baby
Find ways to make it more smooth
Can't complain?
But it's s-till burning
Capitalism setting that divide
Making everyone pick a side
Some won't even decide
Controlling your wants
Putting you in a jar
For that dream house or car
Making your identity your wants
Capitalism plays on your psychology
Worked your entire life
Saved up for that vacation
Got inheritance
Now what- donation?
Capitalism is the mass religion
Camping outside a store
Obsession with something limited edition
They got you trapped in a cycle
Making you a wired psycho

Doctor am I-

The way these notes play
The way the sky dazes today
Such a peckered kissed slap jumping joy
To be so playfully light
The music makes us swing all night
We are creative creatures to enjoy
We sit complementing
I want to be understanding
Is the blush in my face
A trait of beauty?
Doctor, you've mastered your craft
Do you see it as a developing disease?
Doctor you know all the facts
Do you want to ruin what attracts?
I am only a brain, flesh to bone
I am only input, muscle to output
Is it wrong of me?
To feel so much more?
We rearrange these notes to express ourselves
To be known, to taste, smell, touch, cry, die
We have something to prove
Or improve the very quality of something
Makes you filled with fancy
So much whimsy and awe
Bursting out like a giggling child
It's not mild lets go wild and play
It's so aesthetic today

You are the ghost behind the scenes
Little drama queen
Lost all knowledgeability
Lost within hierarchy
Running around with a smile
Running within naivety
Your mind runs with ego
Blind little bird hitting the window
Splattering my thoughts
It is stiffing with your words
Birdie leave me be
But I kindly let you in
Fooled by the ghost behind the scenes
Short hair
Short skirt, checkered shirt
And a wild sultry stare
Why should I care
You were always such a teacher's pet
I admired that till I was the test
can say you disgust
But you are oddly so pure
If everyone can cause the chaos you do
Without a care
Everyone would be so happily true
Why don't I hate you?
Tricked by the birdie
Constricted so firmly
You only know luxury
I let the ghost in

Strawberry surprise
The sunlight was striped in my room
Warmth so welcome on my forehead
But the concrete was hot with anger
And the shadows whispered me in
With ill intentions
The labyrinth hallways felt so claustrophobic
The bell ringed so catastrophic
My tears swelled
And I felt like a slushy inside
A frozen inner pipe so guilty
sweetheart
You stood in a field of sunflowers
Pulled me in and held me a way I've never been before
Your embrace made me shake
But you reassured me it was okay
Wrapped all your pressure onto me
My heart was secure in concrete
I always wrote to you my words of adoration
One day you returned the favor
Your letter said I always kept on giving
Said I was a warm bowl of chicken noodle soup on a rainy day
Felt so alive I made you feel such a way
But my heart let out a bloody scream at the end
Your own words said
You were a rose with thorns…
I was so troubled you felt such a way
strawberry
I woke up the next day…
All the sunflowers were dead
My hand now covered in thorns
Hey strawberry…?
What happened?

Everyone is so full of shit
They'll even agree with it
But at the end enable it
Fearing not much to be said
Just are five gaping holes
The embodiment of tooth decay
Making jaws hurt
Wanna be chained up
No sense of self control
Such a dark sickly culpability
Discovered self worth in others
A mind a maze
Wanna free them all
Everyone is such a gall
A mushy haze
Give enough for a little wannabe squeeze
Wasting so much opportunity
Nobody here gets out alive
Unless you have the desire to survive
Dunno wether to kill myself or you
Stumbled up something
Pure fun and lost connection
Just raw desperation
Some room with men swinging it around
Whip cream covered snakes
Did they want to be fucked numbly?
The morning comes it is forgotten so calmly
Till the fucking comes the next night
And it is so loved
Returning to the modern office
Drinking that best dad coffee
Rolling her wedding ring
So much hidden behind the surface

1 2 3

1 2 3, Apollo-woah, 2 years ago you were in the position
I am in now
1 year ago, I was just like those people
You where in that place
3 years ahead of me
Still the same
The bodies just grown
Ideas set in stone
Placement in this room
Hundreds have before
Sitting by the place we kissed
It is simply too surreal
While I cry on a log
All the time I lost
But I never even knew you then
You mentioned it years ago
This place
And now I am standing here
But cannot tell you
1 2 3, Apollo-woah, got so jealous, so focused
Wanted to be significant
Be able to prove myself
Now that I am here, the faces look babyish
It really wasn't that serious
Felt so intertwined with you
By a life I never lived
Long ago you played here with friends
I swore I could still hear them laughing
Shivered when I saw your initials
1 year, 2 year, 3 year, must reclaim memories here as my own
Apollo-woah, a short period of time on paper
It felt as if you were experiencing a completely different galaxy
It was infinity ago, like I missed something that can't happen again

Sweetest cherry you drench my innards
With pure content
Making the most wet room, so dry
Like the morning dew after a night in a canvas tent
The tricks the mind plays on you
Quivering lips shaking core, it overwhelms
Like a brick against a wall
Cozy and heavy, walking around awol
Perhaps like an old charming romance movie
The goal is to make you all woozy
Awaiting your face only a certain day
The day you fall into my arms
Fall heavy to carry your weight
This human connection
Rolling around on the floor before
Was forever associated with the past
Like it was all some fevered flesh
But this is fresh and sweet
Heartbeats sharing a beat
Up at night, must be in your dreams
A mop of hair laid beside on the mattress
Two hearts rhythmic
You are as rich as raspberry dark chocolate
Cherry never thought this mold would fold to fit
A girl like you, For you are nourished and full of life
Just oughta tell the world about you

A pitch black bus ride to shelter
The traffic lights and high brights flare through rain
Gently admiring through the window
The morning concrete glisters wet
The air is chill and crisp to my lungs
Chest racing because you await for me
Do you remember the little details?
That photos will never be able to recall
Luckily I have a memory
But that's not documentry
The spring air as snow melts
Hearing the water run through the creek
Purple morning skies, navy mornings, the pink ones, orange highlights
Drops on the nose, to my soaked shoes
Humanity, why do we deserve to experience such wonder?
Yes it is just a dress you see, but it was supposed to be next to me
Whatever happened to the red scarf?
Given to you, you wore it with a grin
Now I feel so grim
The pain I can't share our memories
Pumped with bliss, without shame
The pictures now discarded
But I regret they are gone
Luckily I have memory, not documentary
When I die it'll be gone, the way I felt for you
The violets, reds, lavenders, burgundy
That was how you made me feel
Pictured in my head
Im behind hugging you
And you hold onto my arms
Grinning against my throat
And my chin on your scalp
Never letting go

And you are wearing my red scarf
I no longer have that picture
So it is repeatedly described in the head
Luckily I have memory
But it is not documentary
Dreaming there's a sunset
I have to say goodbye
Looking out the back window
There you are staring
And we look with such love
But that is not reality
And when I die
All this love will break out
Maybe I'll reach you again
Memory floating
All the pictures gone

A Man Hungry, A Man Angry

Removed the right of body, no father
Another child born into foster
But they say work yourself up
Trapped into jail, into system
Another number in the lineup
A man hungry
Is a man angry
They say it's all self choice
Saw the embodiment of poetry
The homeless man sitting
Saw beauty in everything
He was somehow the richest man in the world
A person just wants to be appreciated
He appreciated the temperature for it appeals
For it meant he still feels
Staring up at the cloud, he is dreaming
Undying lust seeing people share new hopes
Confiding in another passion boils
His body was stone the next morning
Dead with a smile
He died so rich
He was lustful for the beauty of transcending
Beyond the pavement of mortal impurity
Being humble is not thinking of yourself as less
But simply thinking of yourself less
The genuine desire to be integrated with another
His compassion for life reduced stress
He was bless

I wanted to be a romantic writer
A thoughtful thinker
But how to be a diplomatic fighter?
A crazed biter
Remember lipstick stains, Can you?
My expectations are classic value
Yet all this pressure and regret reside
A boy who had intentions of purity tied
What are his maturities?
And insecurities?
My mind isn't wired to tolerate
The state of our desire
My Sire, A troubled child in the body of a man
Delivever, A lifestyle ending in her life
Already mourning the people alive that once nurtured
If you'd see through my eyes
I saw a porcelain face so sweet euphoric
You didn't give the way I do
Your mouth faked "I love you"
To experience touch, small hands delicate
No more to give it was stolen
I'm cold and calculating now
Statistics shown, the menu is systematic death
Every 20 years, another reset
Always a group advocating
Another slaughter from a preventable threat
Caring for and adoring before
Everything I've dreamed is ashore
Got nothing to lose anymore

Like a warm lamp, the walls glow with something peculiar
When she was only a child
Dark espresso wood so fatherly
Chocolate bark melts on her tongue
Smelling the chestnuts
She cuts her wrists for she feels
It is deserved…
Blood contrasted white tile
The lights buzzing
So sickly, silent ocean sight strandedness
Slept for days head felt cooked
Emotional underdeveloped cackling leaks
Like that spot between his legs
How can she find the power?
To end all things learned tonight
It is the raw guilt she feels
Does she remember happiness?
Open the cloudy pillow for the rag doll
Something more has to be a factor
Before all this nastiness
Never allow this to happen to her, sweet child
The world was not worthy for her purity
Seeing her dance wild with a grin
Seeing her dance wildly in the summer

"I hate you"

"Excuse me?"

"You say you care yet you don't go that extra mile"

"You'd be nothing without the stuff I've given"

"But you give items, not time. Items for my independence. We have limited time, independence can wait"

"You'll be over this tomorrow"

"My feelings are valid and real, you spend your life isolated with material joy sipping high class beverages pretending it is not some decoy compared to the millionaires given it all. You are too self centered to even include me in the time you do have, simply wouldn't work. You are lazy in that, yet slave away hours for bare necessities. The tokens of appreciation you show are stickers on the actual problem"

...

Both became space dust, lost in time. Decades in distance apart.

Autumn Hair

When I first saw you
The leaves were turning colors of fiery
Autumn matched your hair
Wearing a dress of roses
My favorite for proposes
You became such a good friend
Then winter came, needed warmth
Rubbing my ice hands
You said hold my breasts
Eating our ice cream after the show
You ended the night with midwest's scream
Our hearts decided it was time to grow
And you collapse into my arms
You drove me home
Kiss in the car park
It was always so dark
Everything was so freezing
Yet our hearts warmed the other
Then the wonderful bubble popped
Left all alone when the clock change
The time you would of taken me home
Everything was not night, it was bright
And it felt so strange in daylight
It was so comfortable in the dark with you
Despite it being brittle and jag
I'd stare at the oven setting sun
Toughen through the act of being stag
Wish I was still in ice
Forever I'll pay the price
Now it is autumn again
Staring at the trees of fiery
My care for you emulates
Into a spectrum of sharp lines of numb

White poles that impale my very soul
The sight of your ugly face makes my eyes water
The waves of a stage
With wooden boards
Cozy red and brown, layers of paper
The dates aren't matching up, feeling very rare
We existed anyway
Both ended up on the same highway
Beautifully haunting, old dusty air
Now nothing to do with me
Times have changed for our love
The winter is gone
The flowers bloom
But the heat will never be warm like you
We danced in the cold
So bold while we hold
You'd spin and laugh, give it back
Your aura haunts my mind
Give the moment back
The ghost of the last waltz
Was it just false?
Times have changed
It crashed so deranged
The dance that brought us close
So cold today the weather didn't matter much
But the warmth of memories becomes lonely
Hundred years or more with you so homely
Shouting was crying
Be honest about why you walked away
People change every day
From the way you'll talk to the way you carry
To me though, it'll be like the first time
When leaves turned colors of fiery
A warm touch of reminiscing
Yet still the first time

Property Of Body

What to do what the body
Is money, stripped of mind
Got no respect for the property of body
Ran into in the alleyway
Ever seen your organs?
Put it bluntly, no longer seen as human
Harvested for pure gain, killed for innards
Infants disappearing off streets
Why, die softly
Walking around sucking air
Lung not yours
Original had life sucked early
Government scrapping people
Horrifying no longer seen as a soul
Just flesh and bone
Good stuff scooped, rest of husk dumped
What makes you a person, killed for innards
Own citizens just profit
Vomit covered pillow
He bites down onto it, this is for your own good
The white room, stump finger dragged bloody marks
Listen to the little boy's plea with a bruised lump
Was that a hand in the trash bag?
Keep your mouth shut or you'll end up bad
Slaving for hours for being bullied
Digging a grave fitted for a babe
All the young sweat they gave
How is the fucking freak married
Sending her 50,000 yearly
But that ain't even his skinny salary
Guess why people are disappearing off streets
Red market of magical healing
Eat the eyes to see better

From the alleyway she is pulled
The authority listened while she was murdered
Her final words murmured
300 plus equal chunks
Not diced, but skinned and sliced
Packaged and shipped
He got rich

Tonight is time to let you go
It wasn't long ago
Use to fight for you so deadly
But your smile with him is steady
And it made me feel peaceful
Like you did long ago
It is time to rest
Sinking into nothing more
To obsess or press
It is finally shut, the door
Keeping me on solid floor
You are nothing to me
Finally
Rest easy today love
For it's just chemicals in your brain
You are curled in a shivering ball
Manically pressing keys
And feeling the squeeze
Of knowing the pressure
Gets no fresher
Rest easy today love
For it's just the circumstance of the moment
The words of constructed control
It's just the chemicals in everything

Why is an angel like you questioning your beauty?
Each stroke is intentional by the creator
Made by people that loved each other's faces
You are my favorite piece of art
Bones a custom chassis
Skin your own exterior
Simply the way you turn to look at me
I see abstract depths of twirling color
Your voice a symphony of other worldly ambitions
Kissing the marks on your skin only you can give
Those were the days, pushing you in a shopping cart
We'd never part, unreal to feel the warmth of another
The man buying a Valentines Card said, he loved love
We ran away giggling
Your sadness, face in my chest you cry
Fool abandoned you so cruelly
Will I ever compare? He couldn't see inside
Have to protect you till the day I die
But can't even drive you home
The tv lit room watching a film
Breaks my heart you feels the character's pain
Yet I forget the plot
As you pull my hair to learn why the neck
Is the greatest human weakness
Holding your face it is angelic
Pulling me into your mind
Your eyes make me cry
Wrote a song it was too long
Writing all of this in your story
Can only retell it poorly, abstract depths of lore
Drowning in a gorgous coral reef
Every Time I saw you weep, I cried
Every Time I saw you smile, I sighed

This is not a confession of love
"You suck as an investment
Got my own priorities
Working up to befriend the authorities
Got to seek my own securities
Maybe money does buy happiness"
This is not a confession of love
"Nevermind the minorities
Mini wars in first world countries
Obviously never worked with a tie
You can always sell your body
Us businessmen need to buy
Because I don't understand any soul
That isnt my one of green payroll"
This is not a confession of love
"Got a mansion, with multiple televisions
So I can watch us blame the people
That we damned
Swiping so calmly
Time for some molly"
Leasure of pleasure and shelter

Look at her go with that new dress
I'm becoming an emotional mess
Trying too hard to impress
When I really should confess
The process goes, I could be happy
I'm an animal that cries over memories
Id hold you if I could, no worries
You are unquestionably special to me
However someone kissed me first in the dark
And it lit a spark
Won't fall into this generation's stupidity
True romantics don't say I love you for fun
Victim of an addict of kisses
Perhaps you where too
Because I feel like I haven't before
Like a kid in a candy store
Though is it just science I'm experiencing?
No fictions of fate, just questioning
Who do you trust with your deepest pain?
Recite I don't care, it's all fair
I'm becoming an emotional dress
Trying too hard to impress
When I really should confess

Psychedelic Canvas of Conception

What once was a zygote
Now I am aware of everything
My own identity
But all my cells have died
Been replaced instantly
I am not the person
That walked yesterday
Once an aimless biomass
But my soft baby brain has converted
Be now a psychedelic canvas of conception
You are psychically not your old self
Every single second cells die within yourself
Becoming replaced with new ones
So no matter what you regret tons
You are scientifically new
But still have all the features knew

You still remember the night- the black sky
Contrasts with penetrative store lights buzzing by
Your hand on her thigh
You don't know how this conversation started
But don't wanna hear what she and him did
In the back of her car your sitting in
It's not the desire to control, you just feel for her so
All the things you wish you could of undid
Her clothes hide everything you saw
Was taught a woman's body is a temple
Trusted you with her beauty marks so it's law
And you will be warmed by this fact
But do be warned, you've fallen very deep
You won't be able to ever let her go
Now you've attended between her thighs
Her faded drooled dreamy eyes
Where full of adolescent misjudgment
Her mouth around your thumb
Rolled around your tongue pedal
Don't give into nature so easily
It was your care for her deliberant
Her soft body before- so angelic made of clouds
Lips so warm heart so rapid for what?
Nature? People off like a prom dress darling
You simply don't lose a friend, no betrayal
You just never talk again
The soothe twinkle of her eye
She was an investment of true aim

Echoing beyond the grave
Heard a little girl cry
Walked forth, seeker of lore
Into a cemetery world, where stories explore
Symbols of hope in a somber, sacred space
Guardians of children on their journey unknown
Their wings, soft condolences, heavens they've flown
This cemetery, a book of stories untold
Where skeletons keep secrets, young and old
Under moon's soft glow, their mysteries reside
In the whispers of dreams, they forever bide
It was all so still
All the stories now complete
Under the feet
Now no more meat
But a cry is heard, seen in the eye
It is the blue shallow stance
Shattering all memories of joy
She shambles because she is dead
All bled, bullet in the forehead
If only you had known the future that awaited
You were adored
All your thoughts forever stored
Shot in the head by someone misled
Now go lay in the grassy bed
Where flowers sprout from your head
To grow tomorrow, echoing beyond the grave

Slumber of odd
Yet chimeric feelings
Out of this world sensations
Dreaming in my little pod
Of bumbling chemicals
Have not seen any of this absurdity
Warm love, fear, anxiety, absolutely
Colors I've never seen before
How so hazy, hazy, hazy
I know I wont remember anything
In the morning
Will cry for it has ended
That was all so unprecedented
It is lost, lost, lost
Gone, gone, gone
Can never dream of such things again
I'm sorry my brain is so lost in separation
Can not put it back together in disfigured union
Will always try to remember
The hazy waves of emotion and color
And for all characters lost
I can not remember your form
Yet I'll remember your presence
Remember not your traits, but the possibility
We met
Back into the physical realm, I go
A random thought occurred
It was just the visage while you spoke
Remembering sensations
Ditching solid momentary experience
A conflicting and hard pill of nostalgia
Yet it settles peacefully
I'm floating with high frequencies

Like my soul feels too much
And it just wants to escape
It wants to forget it's self
Torn into fragments
Of ever deteriorating memory

The paper house has been lit
Watch the people cheer over it
Last month was fireworks
Now it is waterworks
It started with one gun shot
Than everyone fought
Last week was talk of golf
Now the whitehouse has been engulfed
Listen to the people cheer
As the people who were killed on this land
Don't know wether to laugh or cry
As the killing continues in vain
If only a group had a better plan
To not make decades go to waste
All the hardships overcome
Just to light the paper house
All empires must fail
You were never safe, even with webbed news
Only if someone led with depth and not enforced views
Not money or sheer power
Someone who experienced pain
Felt their weight on buried bones
Under great plains suffered for gains
Only if someone didn't pull the trigger
But instead caused change with pure love and vigor

A Beautiful Day To Admire

A beautiful day to admire
The accomplishment of all that exists
Death, corruption, war and more
Though it all bothers me
Realize it isn't fate and happiness is really equal to pain
At the end of the day everyday is a beautiful day to live to thrive or shuffle to fight
The chances of feeling trapped or free are very equal
Despite the circumstances I feel it isn't fate and we have the power to overcome
All that lived in sweat backed neck broke brown water wells to drown
It is well, so swell. Because despite that being their reality, now they are asleep.
None of it reaps
Everyday you leave your house, smile or frown, hope or envy
No matter- equal chance to die from a car
What a beautiful day
Flowers full of color, some shriveled
Lovers embrace together, others lonely and lost
Grand buildings, others crumble to dust
All equal, not fate
Take the ugliest equal to the beauty
Staring at your hands profusely
Some create, or destroy
Others see life clearly, or foggy
Some self love, or self hate
Flowers full of vibrance, soaking up the goddess sun
The all mighty sun gives so much power
One day it'll blow, destroy everything
Will we be long gone?
No need to dread
Because once our earth, mother, long and gone, it won't matter
So it is a beautiful day to admire what we have
Make most of it, be your own god
Control your life being grateful for all your aches
Overtime it may change, but now it is reality

All is well, so very swell
Everything exists for we do
A lot for bad, but for good
The sun gives so much, but will be the ultimate taker
All is swell, so well
Let us admire all that exists

Fuel feeling up my chest
Burning through so real
Neon city lights so surreal
Wet grass smell on a foggy hill
And a penetrative wall of forest green
Enter the world of ever conifer
And the road is rough in this normal neighborhood
Where children ride their bikes
Wind chimes in the wind
Breeze blowing while I sit on steps
And I feel it all through the cracks
And all the lives through bricks around me
Times like these
It is truly seen Im functional, very aware and well off
But like a broken screen, it sometimes won't compute
And my hardware glitches a feeling
The way that person behaves
The way that situation played out
Makes me feel like a moldy box
On dirty carpet, smoke filled air
Beer bottle smell
Like a dirty rug a creeped static tv
A lightless house lit by windows
Erect disturbed floating down
Anxiety bouncing around within hollow chambers
The setting I am in reminds me of another time
Where a critical hit was struck
An injured animal limping on a ragged leg
Into a inclined dirt road, dead tree canyon into darkness
You've lost sense of direction, but know you are falling
Weighted down with something deprived and hungry
It is times like these I see the human mind is terrified

Running through shadows
Nothing shows
Jangly Branches
The barking advances
Orange hue
Only trees anew
The dogs are after
Fear disaster
Traveling it is all the same
Sky is such a opaque flame
Find a void house
Run inside like a mouse
The dogs follow
Will they swallow?
Run to a dead end
It is all only a two blend
The window shows orange
The barking now, will be over

The Sun gives

The sun gives
But will be the ultimate taker
While my heart bleeds
I smile at everything
Dripping everywhere
It's bleeding down the sleeve
Past laughter doesn't just leave
You are the sun girl
A pull into a world crafted by gas
You said you couldn't stand to look at my face
But trusted to have your back turned into me
Your friends all surprised I was back
The things you'd do for a old connection
Apologized for…the things that hurt me
Trying to buy some cake
To make up for being late
Shop announcer talking about
Something so faintly familiar
You took up swept me away
But I woke up
Cannot tell if it is relief or not
Like I finally got the soap out of my eye
And sat with the warm water drizzling onto me
Could not move, I tried
The sheets so lovey and doughy
Pulled me down, the bars a magnet
Eyes forced shut by chained weights
In my dreams where you, You smiled
Woke up again a fish out of water
Head aching with apprehension
Like I swallowed too much chlorine
After being resurfaced
It was just…

To simply look at someone with love
To simply share my food
To sit side by side girl
You'd look at me
Much more easily dreamy
Than the illusions my mind gives all night
It is all fake walls
Just a twisted joke
Or a moment of heaven
Like the nucleus of the sun girl

Your silver studs turned gold and emerald
My black leather turned tan corduroy
We celebrated the feeling of healing
Ah oh I kissed your scars
Though the past was a controller
Turned us so bipolar
Wont turn snowed in like that
Walking where we hugged
Now covered in flakes
No trace of the ones that loved
The date of our kiss approaches
Reminiscing the beach of security
Hot sands was your body on mine
You can't stop my heart from aching
All the ways the rust was breaking
It felt so right, whispers of sincerity
We'd stay up late, than awake
Without a hesitate
Sun melting the ice, crisp flesh flow
How are you so full of spitefulness?
Ah oh, No. I won't be snowed in like that

Time, Time, Time Again

Time, time, time again
Another firearm bought
Another dead kid caught
Another model purging themselves in the restroom
Time, time, time again
A feminine body pressured and shamed
Another bad cop
Public outcry, lost of stock
Now, now, now again
Another helpful cop
Called and shot
Years, years, years more
Of being low priority
Because you are a minority
Forced into poverty
Needing gangs for stability
High and angry at life
Where is my cash?
Now, now, now again
Another heartbroken mother never wakes up
Time, time, time again
Another assault in a studio dressing room
Unknown to the victim, they were groomed
Falsely accused to hang
Make healthy expensive
Buy into fast food
Time, time, time again
Consumerism thrill
Promoting the street life
Another cycle of hate
From petty complaints
Homeless next to houses of grand illusion
The rats sent to camps

Left with no assistance
Doze off into death
The system not can
So we need more narcan
Time, time, time again
History repeating
Mass fear causing world superpowers
Waking, wake, up to clarity
Humans are so powerful
Our physical shells easily make sin
Biological mechanics unbalanced
Will grind, will wear
Time, time, time again
Let's help each other evolve
Only know now, not after
How you feel can be more than biology
Science and spirituality mixed together
All this human want unnecessary
Time, time, time again
Adapt and learn, protect the damaged

You stand the best amongst the rest dear
Attempt to prepare my heart to tear
I can imagine one day you could love me
The way you smile like comfort tea
I'm struck with not finding anyone else
That interesting, so I melt
So it must be just, Yet that is not rational dear
I don't even know your favorite color
But I reckon it's the color of your nails
It's the color of freedom and intuition
Your eyes match your freckles
Making me forget life's fundamentals
This is just too sentimental
Our faces move similarly
Everyone walks out on my master plan, it hurts
Reality they just weren't as grand
Words are far too cheap to be so costly impactful
I'm sorry for the time I called you bland
It was perplex with depth
I walked into setting light from a very dark fright
It smells so good, have I finally died?
Is that perfume my body
They always said decay was sweet
Not morbid babe
I just appreciate beauty so deep
Sensitive to violence like a babe
I think I'm okay dear

Teakwood Mahogany

Teakwood mahogany was your favorite scent
Perfumed throughout the white carpet room
It's now midnight, goodnight
Can't sleep without that mahogany
After our fight
Worked myself up to play with your hair
To show I still really cared
Yet once my hand touched
You looked at me with shock
My heart dropped
Punched a brick so hard
I wanted to break every bone in my hand
Your rejection told me we where done
I was no longer the same man to you
My hand was no longer suppose to comfort you
Just a man, I felt cruel
Not your friend, this was the end
Just before the last touch
That meant so much
Have not missed
The way I did after just seeing you since
The grassy softness to roll and kiss
Walking up to someone to hug
Wrapped up in a rug
Teakwood mahogany was your favorite scent
Perfumed throughout the white carpet room
It's now midnight, goodnight
Can't sleep without that mahogany

Let me take you where the light don't shine
Foggy woods and tobacco shores
The lake takes broken glass
And it washes it to art
"I'm not drunk"
He watches his son from the window
Losing custody, beats his new gal
Collects nazi memorabilia
Goes on the web, watches people get hammered
Not hammered with flesh, beer, or at a nightclub
Hammered with a big metal club
Gets the blood rushing
Something sinister
With those country folk
God bless America
Jesus committed suicide
Was given the power of god
But chose to be criticized
As some example of sins
God allowed
The given son grows older
Mind twisted, warped
The baby was born with cyclopia
She gasps and wants to chuck up
It just- wiggled around like a worm
And died, not cried
That's not my fucking child

Maraschino lips, Venom

Your embodiment was a vast lush green maze
Your kiss was a dip into maraschino cherries
We'd kiss under a pillow, others watched with willow
Now it all feels like a distant fever dream
Was it ever real?
No I cannot be strong
It couldn't of been wrong
I need venom to stop this dream
You stuck your greasy palm right into my chest
And heard the body tear as you ripped out my heart
Watched me flail and pulse like a headless chicken
Remember that snake that escaped?
You where slithering away with my love
Yet I attempted to give you one last flower
A desperate cry for conclusion
He put his hand on my shoulder, I wanted to smile
Yet I couldn't smile no more for terms
I saw you sitting alone with a distant look
No flowers for you and I was a closed book
It's just a fading memory
For the better

Heart Exhibit

"I gotta get out, gotta get mine, help the mind"
"Hush sweet boy all good things come in time"
On this night, hand on chest
Your love is a locked room
She has the keys, he will hold the door
To let it wrap around two
Look at the fresh sweethearts
Sneak out from the dance
He carries her out to romance
Little did she know
Know you want to care for each other's tragic story
Say dodge the bullet, but you are two that collided together
Blind to a friend, she didn't understand
He said, love I'm a museum of compassion
Of everyone I've ever cared for so split
And my heart don't got room for another exhibit
Had to burn a few to lesson the burden
The ashes become transferred in paper word
The lost dream of a wood cabin and a grand piano
For the kids, she said- have that with me
Yet isn't that outdated, I see spaceships
In the sky- I'm ready to become steel and wire
For its evolution, but will I have the same heart?
"Compassion grew so it's true"

Not someone, 4 years in this little room
Going hang myself with a belt from boredom
My ideas happening in my head bloom
Can't afford them
Don't you dare stand in the way of my plans
Persistence, new age romantic
Gender wars so manic
I don't talk, my mind full of history stardom
I'm more concerned of the matters that dwell on
Like what is there to be free if everything is gone
And I was staring at that stream, all sunlit
And it made me sad the people who drank some it
All them years ago where shot
All the miles they had to walk
Protest is back in fashion again
But is it a thoughtful plan? I wish we knew
The perfect way to answer and solve not blurred
To help those charred bodies, never heard
I want all to be beautiful, like your fragile smile
Like the flowers on tree in April
So bright, so short lived, life universal
The people so skinny from all those drugs
No hugs killed by fentanyl
Looking for someone that's insane
Finding it much more sane
Than working for just food and shelter

Falling asleep, my brain dived deep
Found a glass panel
So clear it wasn't there
But it was a fragment of feeling
I've walked so far
My feet covered in blood
Can you hold me up while we dance
My head in shoulder, pillow to cry in
I was strong, I was happy
Others seemed so sad
Made me feel crazy
Million times at the point of wanting death
But still fond of life
Feet covered in blood
Can you hold me up while we dance
My head in your shoulder
Someone gentle and kind
Not filled with angst, the feminine spirit of
The lotus flower
Walking the night
My body feels light
Sand down in my feet, holding me down
Stumbled into a gas station
Stumble out, wondering why I'm out so late
Feel so aimless without you
My brain has swelled like a balloon
And I just drift away
You say love is just a word that can be taken back
Not a souvenir of the future lost
Are all beautiful things in life just fiction?
The danger of believing in story books
My love must of shocked, for it was real
You no longer need me nor see me

This state of freedom is consuming
Not just a boy, but not yet grown
Already felt like things where set in stone
You took a hammer and shattered it
I flutter however when I realize
That hammer hit your own foot as well
And you'll learn
As I search for the lotus flower
You are my lover not dealer
Friend, not enemy
In my wildness dreams, never ever want to be away from you
Taught me everything I know
I paint your crying eyes
My lost fairy
A beacon for my lost ship your face glows
Ran into a picture of us
I turned blue
That moment captured longer
Yet we couldn't last forever
Have to protect myself tonight, have to learn
Even pretty flowers decay
Feeling I have blood on my hands
But you hired me to end your misery
My best fallen angel
It's been awhile since Ive
Stepped out into the cold abyss
Without you, the same planet
Wanted to wine and dine, a orange skyline
With the bleeding taste of cherry licking
It's the healing time
Understanding why you had to go
But I am crazy so, to cry over something set in stone
It's the healing time, I will focus on my world
Become a better version of things established
Be more shaded and lush

I am strong and beautiful
Loving myself and my world
Searching for the lotus flower

Standing On a Flower

Standing on a tower
It sent me so far
The pressure crumbled it
The tower shattered everywhere
Then the people around me
Stole its pieces
Build entire kingdoms
From my loved tower
Then the kingdoms started to fight
To steal each other's pieces
Extend the territory
It got so scary
Gazing at a tower
It stood so tall
And if I admired it from a distance
It wouldn't fall

A gun needs a mind
A mind needs awareness
Sin is a urge
A urge needs a mind
A mind needs conscious
Pain is a feeling, awareness
A chemical reaction
With no actual punishment
For life us a illusion
We did not choose this
The weight of situation is non-existent
Because you are the one adding
All the human construct
Nothing is important
Drop your ego
Drop your pride
Live privilege or poor
If you are poor it was not fate
Rich men aren't special
Finding meaning in everything is empty
Or you'll deprive yourself finding answers before everything

Clean Teeth

He prides himself in clean teeth
Though does dirty teeth kill?
When he dies
Was that time spent brushing teeth important?
Will his skull be dug up
And his teeth admired?
Chose to disown and accept
We all die, but so little live
The future is now
Send us to the cloud
Fascist control no more
Death so normalized
Join the statistics
We feel guilty when we feel free
Yet, we live in fear for when the worse comes
Nearby hidden in fees
Evolution is uploading us to the cloud
Thought control
Human body no longer trapping your soul
Don't live to waste
Hate inform you, had to disown you
Love the old you
That cared for the old you
No more calcium teeth
About time you invest into a shiny arm
Steel rib cage
And plug in eyes
This is how you are going to survive
Humanity's slow suicide
You gotta work harder to survive
Gotta buy a fake wife and husband
Work isn't just necessities for the heart
Because the very air you breath is killing

Are you free condepent on a parasite?
Will help your deteriorating mind
Only you can take those practical steps
All the cultures, different smells
Dead, gotta buy metal to survive
All the producing is causing the destruction
So you buy metal
Stuck in the parasite eating your own feces
Do you really want to buy metal to survive?

Seeing you made me sigh
Forced down a smile when I caught your eye
Like a perfumed breath of air
The bald freshness after no hair
I'd gladly take a hot pot from your hands
My unspoken compassion commands
Believed you were sent to keep me grounded
I know I'd drop all my dreams for you
Become blended in Venus's beauty, time ago
My insides feel butchered and raw
Too ambitious for a purse anyhow
But I craved that stability from someone
The suburban houses lined up like a maze
I look up at the toasted moon sky
On the bottom of the hollow ocean, fish bowl
The school some cave
You where an anchor for my views
Affection causing disillusioned highs
Yet with no longer a tie, it's time to arise
Yet the smell of this room, the mist
Strongest nostalgia, makes me miss
The bugs buzz while rolling in the breezed dip
Between the cool grass and the weeping willow
The sun sets and we stare in silence
No words can explain, your impact on existence
Have not laughed widely since, my chest craves
Compulsive laughter that keeps going in waves
I like the way the bad stuff sounds good
You show pictures of the past with a grin
I sit and wonder because of sensitivity
It's almost like I could feel the very aurora
Of that room, it lingered for years
But I woke up one day without tears

Like it was some fever dream movie
That never happened
You asked what stood out such
And what I said was mental
It was, you wear the same earrings everyday
You are obviously sentimental
Legs ache, arms wobbled
But I don't mind as long
It's near you, because then nothing is wrong
I want to tell you whenever you walk away
I feel disappointed and stray
But I don't know much, as far as I'm aware
You feel the same for another, your care
And I'd rather still feel the butterflies
When we lock eyes

Confident indifference

Feeling confident indifference
Never needed much anyways
Haven't learned enough
But don't need to learn no more
I'm not even an artist, of any kind
I use the right brush for my objective
Don't seek perfection
Whatever finishes my direction
Their obligations
Ruined reading for me
Feeling confident indifference
Simply seek self expression
Can't hide freedom
Their obligations
Make me shrivel
Observing things they wouldn't teach
Waiting for the right answers to reach
The only thing I claim to be
Was pure authenticity
When your physical establishments are gone
The only thing you have left is your mind
Nothing seems that real anymore
I've never felt any innocence
Their obligations put me in a cage
And I'm free today

Still professionalism and hair like a bloodstain
Despite what you say, it wasn't youth
We were embracing the truth
Looking at you now, just like the very first time
When you opened the door
The world crashed against your smile
Yet you say I no longer seem like the same person
We were laughing so comfortably
Than you got dreamy eyes, plain to see
I'm just a bit conflicted, why me?
I tasted your cherry gloss, amiss
Was only a boy who wanted to be worthy
I needed to achieve more, you where a ruby jew
Had to work had to provide for you
Was my new hope secretly snide
You said I always smelt great, so I overhauled
A vision without a plan is what builds loyalty
I'll fly fighter jets high in the sky
For I feel that is awfully symbolic of hope
I'll work till my hands don't work
Have class and everything compared will be crass
Whenever you play that piano solo
I never cared much for that song
Now when I hear it I feel holo
How could you listen to those same songs again
So I'll be gone because I know my worth now
Got myself a warm embrace, that won't go

Castoff Comeback

Remember sitting on the parking garage ledge
Feet dangling off the edge
Remember speeding 120+ or more they said
Will retaliate alone, master my goals, you kicked me
But it simply sent me into the sky
I am a castoff comeback
Just smile, and give the mercy I was not granted
The green field, No words can explain
The cold concrete, as I watched you drive away
It all felt, naturally scared, logical and bleak
The seed buried will grow
Darling you are too elegant for me to understand
It is excruciating, hidden by scents and textures

I am curled up into my warm blanket
The pain of complexion and contraction
Bleeds inside my organic shell
At least I loved enough, to hurt this way
Having this warm blanket to protect
Only you can hurt me in the human race
And I'm glad it's you in this bland space
Emotions sizzle in the morning
Remembering the way she praised
It's terrible, wail and contort on the bed
Everything is morbid and doomed
All because you are gone
Walking down the sunny street
Body feels so put together
Muscles connect to the bone
Heart feels nice and strong
Worked on it forever
See that couple kissing in the car
Her hand on his neck, leaning in for more
That was the spot we…
Confused why it doesn't hurt anymore
Perhaps it was never that serious
Smile and keep on walking

A character with elegance and a skirt
A bright scent full day, upbeat summer beats
They stood right next to me
They didn't recognize me
I looked down my shoulder
I was petrified
Thought I'd have forgotten
Your breathe in my face
Your strut with grace, never stood a chance
Why did we ever have to dance
Because you are almost nineteen
And I'm still some highschool dweeb
They looked up right at me with a smile
But they recognized the scar on my nose
But they remembered my aurora that lacked prose
I was crushing like a school boy
On this sunny day, I never stopped loving
They turned away quickly, devil influence
They still had the same length
But it was straightened out
Was it because I adored your curls?
I remember that night I strapped your heels
Your glasses where no more
Was it because I thought they fitted your grin?
You no longer show your goofy smile
The braces I identified with your grin
Long gone, now I'm happy you've graduated from that
But the makeup on your face
I love the self expression
But everyday it's so heavy on your face
And I remember you said, you did not need it around
Because you felt secure with me
It is not the fact it is all gone

I just wished you still smiled at me with those braces
And the makeup is heavier after the breakup
Your real face not vulnerable
But that is all just the result of passing time
But I wish most of all
You still cared to see
All the same changes with me

Karma Grim Reaper

Bragging of paychecks
Look at the dollar on the floor
We should bet on it
That was not the great American donut
Grub in an apple
Dreaming of digging scalpels
Let's all dabble
In perplex matters
No mortal can decide
The peaceful continent
Tainted by generational hatred
Bleed into the river
The southern moist grass
Swampy abyss
It's the gilded age
Muddy soul, fireflies soak
His head blown open
Tainted by your bias sin
We really wish you'd kill yourself
You redneck funky fucking roughneck
Breakneck yet low tech
You've already taken enough lives
Your brain a sloppy mess of hives
You justify rape and kill tapes
The babies seen as cannon fodder
We want you to get down on your knees
Time to correct your mistakes
A whip in the back for every life
So many slashes it is ripped open
But we see no heart
We cry for what we've done
Because you where a baby once too
Your mind tainted by generational hatred

Though your actions must be disciplined
I hope your karma learns one day
Brought back to die in another war
The mistakes from before
Be remembered as some lesson
Your life tainted by generational hatred
We cry for the raped children, dead heroes, naive dreamers
We cry for this generational illness
The imaginary walls you put into place enforced by punishment
The cries heard across the world it will cause a slaughter out
Hiding secrets, you win or die
Your blood spilt, a happy ending, kinda cute, all the bullets made
No one is left to shoot
Big news, months later it is snuffed out and silent
The silence translates to concealed prison walls
And cold dead once so hot being burnt alive
You killed us you say, over the emotionless clothes we wore
You killed us they say, over who we loved brought joy
You slaughtered us you say, over your naive fear
Now the old folks say back in their day everything was better
Yet tens years before humanity dropped its first apocalypse maker
1945 going about life, wife, work, kids, than hatred expanded
Blew up in biblical proportions of prophecy 80,000 dead
Due to government dread
After you are kissing the wounds, why, guilt?
A few pushes of a button nothing exists at all
You've tested the waters you disgusting dirty tease
Edging the concept of drowning everything

Trash Man

He is in the trash can
Filling up his belly
I tell people about him, but it sounds so silly
The trashman strikes again
Living in the trash can, it is the trashman
Baby can't you see
You'll always be precious to me
Precious like the time of year
Or maybe it is the kind of man
I am
And I feel so happy, feel so well
A new girl makes me feel so swell
Can't you see
Treated a man like trash
Dumped in the trash can
Baby can't you see
You'll always be precious to me
Now I feel so strong
I always will be free
Because we stand out like a jew in the can
We always get the worth again
Ain't so silly being the trashman
Filling up his belly

Sugar cookie smell trapped in red candy wrappers
A head rests on my shoulder content
The rain pours and thunder roars
The flames are warm and break through laced cloth
The tall brown shelves smell of wise words
Old not seen gremlins are hidden in tall stories
That are simply not comprehensible
The paintings all random, stitched together
A pure stream of self expression
It is all only lit by candles
The ceiling toasted escaping into dark corners
This place could be haunted, but the ghosts are kind
They will make you cry, not out of fear, but wonder
Royal tastes sit on my tongue, cherries, cranberry, grape
walking through a maze of life changing knowledge
More than half will always be unknown to me
A old world walnut and masoned stone bunker

Sad Satan

She told him
"How did we become so far apart
You no longer hold my delicate heart"
Does he reach the places your fingers can't?
You regret what has been done
But he is thinking of all the new
Things a boy and girl can do
Your beauty speaks when your lips stay shut
Your family has been calling you a slut
After they saw the test, hoping it was some stunt
I remember when you didn't always smell like
Weed and suburban sex
You use to be able to sun tan
Without him exposing your lighter skinned bikini
He use to open the door for you
Now it seems he shuts it
But hc still opens your legs
"How did we become so far apart
You no longer hold my delicate heart"
Don't go visit him tonight
He has already damaged your life
Go relax with your friends instead
Have so much future ahead
You don't need to play these games anymore
You aren't even his only one
She cries into a pillow, snot nosed
She feels so disposed

Deep Dip

The red eyed glowing deer skull
Is screeching and roaring
Something mechanical and angry
The wet air smell of an old building
Next to the creek of condensing pebbles
Tangled tree blue roots are in the shape of crying eyes
City spunk a shop is below my green, purple, gray concrete
Chemical spilt noir world
Welcome in, but you aren't allowed
Dance in the club, chains out and all
What did you do to it?
Holding the dead baby
Just couldn't do it, I killed it
And telepathic signals from hooked portals
Connecting you to the entire world
And all the insanity can be seen
From a click of a screen
The zombies milked by temptation
House ridden psychopaths
Searching for the next victim thrill
Shooting with a button
Never needing to leave nothing
Destroy it, burn the earth
End our stupidity
I don't want to forget joy

Coffee will be her name
She had coffee bean eyes
And coffee grain specks, on her shortbread body
She had hair I'd compare to honeycomb
And I'd of given up anything to be her home
But comparison kills happiness
Comparison to the future overwhelms
Had to become more for her
So I never asked her out for coffee
But I told myself I would one day
Once I was confident in payday
But I was scared, for she was barely there
Had no excuse to ever see her near
Im sure she never even spoke my name
I never even spoke her name…
So coffee will be her traits
It is a story old as time
Unspoken love, many can judge
I tried, I became strong
Was ready to build a world for two
But she was happy with someone
She had always knew
All I could do was wait
For him to turn her world upside down
So I could fix her frown
But it never happened…
No heroic knight this time
I'm now the wanderer
Wanted the future to be the past never had
I've always been the wanderer
Coffee now all I can do is sing
And hope you never hear, because this not fair to you
I hope you know your smile was sweet as honey

All The Months

These words came to me in a dream
You where on a cover of a magazine
I've cried more tears
Than the hours we spent, all the months that went
Where did all the months go?
Were you even real?
I never hear your name, never in the same grounds
The places we went forgotten
The spaces we met seem haunted
I'll never go back, it hurts too much
Feels as if they were a magical trick
The words where, the months are so empty
You where once just a pure friend
At a time I helped you without obligations
Where did they all go?
The calendar I see as fog
It was much more than a touch, your angel face
It was much more than the words "I love you"
It was the fact everywhere we went, is a memory of you
We painted the floor, we left our mark
And although I got rid of reminders
That brickwall in the far back, behind the curtains
Photos of us happy are in your friend's phone
It is touching many more hearts will love
In the same rooms laughed and cried, when we are both long gone
Where did the months go?
In the dream I remembered what is was like
To see you cry, and I knew I could still love you
Your face found and imprinted in my subconscious
But I chose to wake up to reality, I've come so far
You locked your gentle fingers with mine one last time,
but I had the control to let go

Sand Clock

I walked into the grand cathedral, chandeliers, many shined from the ceiling
That was far too tall, the pits inclining tighter and taller
The people wore white button ups and had church shoes
The stain class was arranged in alien visuals, it glimmered
Down by the alter, a circle is gathered
The tall blind folded gray diapered giant stands in front of my face
The boney witch draped in black web holds the metal hooked cross
Carves loyalty into my head
Tasting iron in my mouth
Back in the old neighborhood, all the grass is gone
It is all orange blowing sand, murky brown sky
A childhood house is abandoned, all the color sucked
The windows broken and rooms empty, all black and white
Like an ancient rock dug up
Down at the end of the road all the sand falls into a sinkhole
A metal building full of molten iron melts from the inside
The hot metal collapsing the support, sinking into the hole
The horizon beyond I see jagged windmills fight the sandpaper wind

A tall painted brown skyscraper looms above me
The air smells like gasoline and pretzels
The amber beams travel up it's side
Art deco lights hang like stars
The gold and black triangles
Jump around the purple pool's side
Wrapped around royal cigars

I actually have a nickname in my head for you
Never called you by it because I feared it was too invasive
It was the kind of name you'd use for family or a long time friend
I said the nickname under my breathe at times
You at times actually annoyed me to frustration
I didn't get how you could be so dry
But goof off and be so loud
I'd call it arrogance
But I knew you had a heart of naive optimism
With sensitive reflectivism
Always had a soft spot for you
Maybe I am just a boy and you were beautiful
But at times I genuinely found you ugly
That was rude, I know, but those ugly times
Where when it seemed you were unhappy
I'll never tell you because it seems odd
It is strange and something that makes me regret
Telling you how deeply I felt
A navy whirlpool sucks me in
It is not manic or sharp
But thick
When I think how I miss but dread you

Red Bath

The man is ready to sleep
In the hotel bed, the blackout curtains
He would feel so well rested tomorrow
He heard a primal groan
He woke up, it was in the hallway
Checked, nothing.
Walked, dropped with shock
The figure covered in shallow cuts was dead
His wife was strangled with underwear
Thanksgiving dinner surprise
He took the knives
Layed in bed with a dismembered head
The house was so normal
So American and lived
The bedroom was a redbath
Once seen he just twitched his eyes
Proclaimed his soul already died
The pictures he made of the children
They have gaping wide jaw ripped mouths
He is a slit wrist son of a bitch child fucker
Their arms are mangled and he gets excited
Fetished and all wettish, cannibal baby killer
I am so disturbed by his puss filled face
Wanna stomp it out, stomp out the sickness

In the velvet cloak of night so deep
Secrets you keep
A canvas pink a moon's soft glow
Your prominent endless flow

A midnight hue,
Mysteries wrapped in shades of blue
Kissing to escape the nightmare
A time for reflection, a world laid bare

The city lights, an inspired sight
Grooving in the color of night
Cupcake, don't go back that sad way
In the peaceful stillness we'll stay

The night unfolds I won't misplace
Embrace your mind and trace
The wonders killed by bright light
In the enchanting, ever-changing color of night

Is wanting more- The desire to be my full self?
Or someone else?
Should I stay confused about a roadside rabbit?
Or go find something extravagant and ethereal
White face and blue glitter shadow
My mind was popping with cotton pink clouds
Right after the darkest black and red filtered view
The radio plays angry thrashing guitar
I read the news of this city
It's the "United" states, what can I say?
Can I be that comforting bed in a dim room
After a long day in the cloudy rain
You snuck into the face I was drawing
leave me be
I figured it's time I get some TLC
deserve to experience the happiness you've had
Because I waited forever
And you were just playing no care whatsoever
You've smeared any reminders of me
But I remember when you drew a portrait of me
And I know I deserve some TLC
But maybe one day you'll remember
What you saw when you drew me
So sweetest angel stay out of my dreams
with layers of tactics, cozy drawings never seen
With your new girl, I saw you crying on that swing
Was it because I was still wearing that ring?

Theater Lights

When the rainbow lights shine
I remember what it was like
To stand and watch the fresnels
And across the stage you stood with your arms cross
That once opened up to me
And everyone sang and it ended with clapping
And I'd stare at the led flashing rainbow spectrum
To find something more pretty than you
I should be over it now
It was so long ago
But it still makes me feel so strange
Whenever I smell the forgotten props of a highschool theater
And the catwalks that made you feel easy to fall but valued
She was sitting in the corner so gentle and discreet
Looking so so sweet
A wooly teal sherpa rug in the center of the squeaky floor
Just sipping tea, from second hand china cups

I like those late night deep dark thoughts
That leaves you in the clouds
Glowing fairy blue orbs around my bed
I like those haunting stories
With never a clear answer
Demon red skulls, above my head
And maybe things could of been different
But nothing was set, nothing is preventable
I like the spirits watching me from the woods
They seem so sad, but they live with moss and creeks
And they play around the ancient oak trees
And wonder was killed
By the need for more
Why would we need anything else?
Let's all enter the abyss and find out
And a lady eating tropical fruits
Lays out on the sand before a waterfall
I hear the chants and the animal hide drums
And a man walks a Christmas street
He feels the hot chocolate go down his throat
I see his breathe before the stringed fairy glows
On the oak trees before loving homes
That leaves you in the clouds

Carnival Ghost

Yes he can shred
But has he ever written you a song
And bled
Strumming so slow
Because love built to not collapse
Will always last
I miss you, who is kissing you?
You probably think you are too cool
And I know it's true
Let go of my hand in a carnival crowd
My fear contrasts with the smell of hotdogs
And people arm to arm laughing
And as the sunsets
I never found you again
Fearing I'd become the carnival ghost
Trapped in time
Hearing warped tuncs and empty wind
In dead brown grass fields
All alone
The corn mazes of the East

Into the darkest
All I see is your face
What we've done is so magical
No longer feeling disgraced
And choices are plenty
So why does it sting
And I'm looking for an answer
Within your glance
Such matters are often cancer
Did it ever have a chance?
And the different things people bring
It is so heartbreaking
Into the darkest
You are so breathtaking
I was so free before
Now you hold the keys
To open the door to me
Or set me free

Dickey's

Sunday or so my family would go down to Dickey's
Ten minute drive or so
I'd always get the same sandwich
The bread would scratch your throat
But the pulled meat was seasoned great
After my little sister and I would get free ice cream
Always had free ice cream regardless of day
Small little cones not far off from thin cardboard
But it would wash down the hearty sandwich
West virginia mountains would be in sight, deep green fantasy isolation
Appalachian trails
Spooky black bears and critters chirp
Mountain country is beautiful
We take for granted how diverse the geology of North America is
Silent little decrepit town
With a Dickey's

It feels so numb
News, Murder, Guns
How does it happen
When will it be me
When will it be ones I love
The horror show of mass slaughter
Militant force, the news now silent
How aren't we competent?
We all experience the same touch
What do the others feel within
Don't they also have skin?
Someone just went berserk
Shot the office clerk
Someone just wrongly parked
The outcome was not all bark
Thankgod I'm only watching it on tv!
Wait, that was five minutes near me…
"The public statement will be made
It was the same words used yesterday
Nothing said can amount to this tragedy
Everyone prayed
Send condolences to the family"
"A man with a gun is a citizen. A man without a gun is a subject."

Tell it to the child's splattered brain matter.

I've been lit on fire
Flames a common metaphor
It has happened to so many before
And it gives this motor energy
Gotta stomp into the ground
Time to be found
Wanna get to the city
Gotta get to LA?
Gotta get to NY?
The same dumpster fire in the end
Gotta marry an artist with a life?
Gotta marry a stable housewife?
But young love is forgotten with distance and time
And sparked again with just the eye
And it gives this motor energy
Do I gotta cry?
Do I gotta shout?
Maybe I just gotta dance and let it out
Am I tired?
Am I inspired?
Shots fired
Cocky confidence is broken
Love is worth more than tokens
Where do I belong
Am I accepted?
Am I understood?

I remember sitting in silence
Waiting for you to get home
I felt my skin tighten
So frighten, the tech reflected off darkness
The possibilities of you dying
Did make me feel anxiety all clammy
The complications it would have for everyone
The guilt of the ones you drove from
My anger for I don't have others
I was given time with care
And knew someone paired
He learned too soon she was impaired
I would like to believe I am free from the grasp
Of fondness and adulate attention
I want to be a sociopath
Why is everything so bleak
Don't want to eat and screw
What is there to even do?
I feel so close to you
Be intrusive I feel wrongly
Just awkwardly guilty
I want to think with logic
No connections cause no distractions
A true love is like a friendship
Or so I should just keep a friend
My euphoric state lasted days
I could not sleep, maybe I felt healthy?
No way the passion so tempting was good for my health
I want your soft face in my teeth
The day you deject
is the day all I knew left
But altruism is the biggest way to make profit
Researching the path I'm imbalanced

It was December 2022
We and our friends had fun I'd say
Tarot reading within the adolescent place
I was always drawn to you and your observing face
Mentions of a miscarriage at times made me judge
 But something about you I just couldn't nudge
And your reflective globnose smile was so pure and raw
And I knew I could never judge
Because you settled like fudge
A deal with myself I'd care for you
Suffering under your converse shoes because it's right to do
But I spat my ego up
Put you high priority when your so called friends
Left your name in the gutter, wanted to helped cleanse
And by January 14th I was wiping lipstick flecks
Don't remember what else happened that month
But by the 27th I dare say
I had you bare and I, Haha, the other pair.
After you said you were deeply in love
But under your crimson waves exists a brain
And it was pumping with convolutedness strain
Your body touched by boys misled
Saw my doting eyes as a snake instead
Remember we laughed like high crazed newly weds
Wish I understood sooner your fragile beating pulse
Wish I took the time to be patient and not divulse
And by December 2023 you were just a flashed moment in time
I don't need you, but I am forgetting the feel of unconditional love
Standing in autumn plucked Pumpkin fields all alone
Seeing the campfire smoke in the dead trees, close but unreachable

The oil is spraying in a pressure chamber
People are shredding from voices of anger
The preppy step can seem so real and viel
But forgets in a day and rolls away like a wheel
The confidence of yesterday is dying
Today I saw the only buddies back turned crying
Someone has been constantly bitching
And you gotta run or your fixing a stitching
And I witnessed this in a day
The sudden flips cause so much dismay
And it makes your stomach weak
Makes you want to shake all week
And the diplomate is stuck in the middle
Stuck between logic and care
safety in the resit of biologic need or fist fulls of hair
The anorexic thing is bent down so low dancing
sharp elbows stick from the ulna and radius thrusting
The long pointy teeth crooked out
long dead scalp centipede strings down to the waist
sneezed before it's head fell off
And it started to seize
I wanted to reisure it's dead liquid filled body
And it was so long gone, not human
What has mother nature done?
The oil is spraying in a pressure chamber
People are shredding from voices of anger
The preppy step can seem so real and viel
But forgets in a day and rolls away like a wheel

Tell Me, Is Love Free?

Divorce.
"Do you remember how you got that bruise"
No.
"From your dad"
Daddy and the new girl fight and throw
He took me on a lake walk
"Have you eaten?"
But Mom, I'm not hungry
"No, I mean have you been beaten?"
My dad played T-ball with me
I don't…remember
I won't be like him
Will I die loved and remembered?
With a gentle lady to share memories
To offspring
Or die
While my leaves are plucked stiff
Feeling still aborted
It happened, fifteen
"Your so fucking hot"
I am? That's sweet.
"Says the guy that thinks we are actually watching a movie"
Her pelvis slips and grinds over my lap, my neck attacked
"I love you" rolled off her tongue
Giggling, exploration, nature walks alone
4 months later she was no more
Last thing I heard, Give it a day
Was it love? Turned on its side?
How can you walk from crying eyes?
Stuck up sour…poor girl, I feel for her
I hope her heart is protected by someone new
I've forgotten love is positive and free

Memories in black cube particles away
Piled upon others in this gray checkered slate
What have I done?
Why do I feel so numb?
When you view the world
As atoms and needs
It scares you when you just don't care
Why do I no longer cry over the fear ridden?
The ones scared brutalized to statistics
I need to feel
Can you make me remember?
Remember moral high ground
I once said maybe it was smart to view
Everything as meaningless
But a friend said that was pitiful
And I agreed
I saw lovers, flowers, sweet desserts
money…concrete…memories of the dead
I don't want to die
Can you make me feel?
Please it is my birthday
Don't ruin what I know
Everyone Mother fucker betrayed her
I hate you all
You have to seek the resources
She isn't capable
Tied down in a psych ward bed
I wish you'd put a shotgun barrel in your mouth.
So I can watch your watermelon pop.
Heaven is near, no more fear, heaven is near
Angels softly sing
Seeing no shades
No biased association of connection

Everything means nothing
Floating in blackness
Not warm or cold
No weight felt
Hearing no ringing
What was before God
What was before the big bang
A thousand specks of souls

The whale washed ashore
Watch the guts pop on the floor
I'm leaving the sleepy pouters behind
All they do is act declined
The road feels good and firm
And I'm looking real, feel it
I'm looking good
People and their lies
I gotta minimize
Fix some lose ties
And her name means royal fabric
On my side
And my deck is becoming full
On the nose bridge
Everything is making sense again
Mr. stop your complaining
And I laugh at your numb surprise
Baby don't you see reality?
We don't need no conspiracy
To know everything is screwed
Time to let loose
The whale is washed ashore
Watch the guts pop on the floor
Feel your face glaze over
Don't go back to the chair again
Money dont grow on trees
But trees grow your air
I'm leaving the sleepy pouters behind
All they do is act declined

Ant Farm

Sure create, you primate
It processes the mind
But can you make profit
You gotta market
All anyone does is move from town
Eat at a restaurant during a trip
Get promoted
See the same animals at the zoo
Someone else is drunk
Life is math with set assets
I can do all of that
What am I missing from the human experience?
Why do I see cars on roads as ants in tunnels?
Networking system of reproduction
We are all one massive ant farm

Hey you in the wind swept dress
Remember how you said I was the best
Don't worry, we've all been longed exed
Your physique short beside him holding hands
I guess it is sweet
now knowing not one experience I've had is unique
the last time he called you beautiful
Was when your bra was off
Your eyeliner teardrops quickly hidden in the bathroom
 but you say you are well-off
I know I was too far gone when I ran my mouth
Trying to impress you with grand romantic ideals
Things I've been told only woman understand
Do you like me more silent and reserve?
Both sides are the real me, I'm a social chameleon
Just tell me what you prefer
You say he is your boyfriend
But he does not seem to be a friend
I don't love you, I'm not stupid, But I'd like to
No need to pretend
You ain't even his wife
You need a better life
I don't think life has much meaning
Yeah it's bleak and hopeless
But all beautiful things in life are given
Like you, making me hopelessly distracted
And painfully attracted
Don't settle, Let's ascend, don't want a bitter-sweet end

Begin To Think About

It's time to get in a bout
Of thinking about
All the to be things I don't know
But see enough about
They come in constant bouts
All the things from long ago
Things that are yet to show
The only cure is to be numb
Or to be wildly dumb
Because not enough are thinking about
They are just bleeding out
What to do? so little, but time for one
People are harvesting from
And causing long stormy bouts
C'mon it is time to think about
Stop your freaking out

We wouldn't have achieved anything if people just sat
And said "Things are so pointless"
But that is when everyone just sat growing bread
To not be dead
Fashion trends come and go
But we are the animal that wears clothes
And for thousands of years we've sat in homes
I need to find something new
Going put a bullet in my head
It seems like a good way to get ahead
Many people lift weights all day
Many people sing songs to sway
Many people cook away
Many people are just cool
Many enjoy using a tool
What is it to be a human being?
Is it to be full after holding her for hours?
Is it to be empty when she leaves taking long showers?
Is it to begin to think about all the things you've done?
And all the people you miss?
And you begin to hate everything?
When I was kid me and a friend tried digging a hole
It was fun
In that spot it was never done
Somewhere in misty North American land a farmland house crackles
Someone enjoys a view sipping eggnog
I didn't put my soul on sale
Take it out of jail
Make me feel new sensations

So you've crawled through the nest
squeezed through the psychedelic lumps of age
Felt the knives scrape your ribcage
The gravedigger of families
Is simply memories
How can you measure a mundane life?
It is mundane till it is lost
You've crawled through my hive
Are you feeling the need to be revived
Can you now thrive?
Can you when so many did not survive?
Hopefully joy was felt
Hopefully agony
You where made a toy
Witnessed killjoy
Yet you just read this thankfully
How can you measure a mundane life?
It is mundane till it is lost
Knowing trauma is privilege
The lucky ones think
Truly an American tragedy
A brutality, but fantasy
Love is the cure
Life is love
Free of what is above

www.ingramcontent.com/pod-product-compliance
Lightning Source LLC
Chambersburg PA
CBHW070826110726
47973CB00034B/294/J